AF439179

My
Love
to You...

Jonathan Vold

SIMORGH PRESS
2022

My Love to You...

Independently published by Simorgh Press,
900 East Northwest Hwy, Mt Prospect, Illinois

© 2022, Jonathan Vold, all rights reserved.

All cited quotes are shared with appreciation to their sources.

ISBN-13: 9798839403970

My Love to You...

Table of Contents

Love is patient; love is kind;
love is not envious or boastful or
arrogant or rude. It does not insist on its
own way; it is not irritable; it keeps no
record of wrongs; it does not rejoice in
wrongdoing, but rejoices in the truth.
It bears all things, believes all things,
hopes all things, endures all things.
Love never ends.
— Paul the Apostle [1]

---

[1] See page 8.

Introductions

Mo Anam Cara

i.

Dedication

Dear Friend,

This is a book about love. It directly follows two other books, one on hope and one on faith, each written and compiled with this third book very much in mind. In other words, those books were about love too. Or they were stepping stones to where I wanted to go, supports for what I want to hold up high, or the warmup for what I really want to say.

And this is to you, my closest friend — mo anam cara, as I would call you in Celtic. Or in French: mon ami, mon amour, mon ame. My friend, my love, my soul. I give this to you, anam cara, but also to you who are not yet called my friend, perhaps a neighbor or even a stranger, in the hopes that we may become friends, good friends, faithful friends. This is my love to you.

The first book of this series, My Hope for You, was dedicated to my children. I hoped to reach more than my two offspring, my favorite son and my favorite daughter, with that book but they are who started the conversation and they deserve the credit. I did not name them then so let me do it now: Kirsten and Andrew, that hope book was, and always is, for you.

The second book, My Faith in You, was dedicated primarily to my readers. Believing that faith, more than hope, is something that moves from personal to social, I asked you, dear readers, to not only accept my belief but to help my unbelief.

This third book, My Love to You, sounds like it should be more personal again, and my first instinct is to dedicate this book exclusively to one I have vowed my love to: my wife Cara, whom I love to call my Cara Love.

But I have learned, and my wife will understand, that love is meant to be more than a private valentine. We will always have our vows for each other, but we have been taught to love others as well, beyond ourselves and as much as ourselves: to love one another, our neighbors and our world, our friends and our enemies too. So, mo anam cara, and anam cairde everywhere, I dedicate this book to you.

ii.

A Roadmap

With My Hope for You, I spoke of you,
wanting, not expecting, to connect,
desiring, more than wishing, to believe
and in my turn to be somehow assured.

With My Faith in You, I talked with you,
reasoning and having reasons why,
though never knowing how, we ought to find
our way to truth, our turn to be inspired.

With My Love to You, I turn to you,
feeling, more than knowing, what is true,
believing in the why and learning how.
I've shared all that I have discovered of
my hope for you and faith in you and now,
returning to the source, I give you love.[2]

---

[2] J. Vold, A Roadmap (2022).

There is, I believe, an ultimate source of love, but this book, following My Hope for You and My Faith In You, will turn to many voices to hear what others have said about love and all that it means. As before, the heart of my book will be their words, preserved and shared, but to start things out I would like to propose a roadmap to help us on our way.

It would be nice to just let love and quotes about love happen as they may, but this could be perilous. Love has many sidetracks, like lust and desire, and pitfalls, like broken hearts and misunderstandings. In compiling these quotes I have come across many that dwell on harsher sides of love, with rough edges, disappointments and cautionary tales. Even if we try to leave those words behind us, it is not always easy to stay positive.

Here, in a wandering list off the top of my head, is what I know without a map:

1. Love means many things (affection, devotion, compassion come to mind),
2. and though it seems inexplicable (more than I can put in words or fully comprehend),
3. it is nothing if not expressed (love songs, love letters, professions of love)
4. and lived (experienced, received, given and grown)

5. and shared (projected, not contained, turned from intimate to universal).
6. Whether love is from above (John 3:16, 1 John 4:7-8 and 1 Corinthians 13)
7. or from the heart (Valentine, Cupid, and always more than X's and O's)
8. it comes with a spectrum of intensity (luv, love ya, I'm in love with you)
9. that in the extreme can be a state of abandon (mad love, selfless love, no greater love).
10. Whatever else, my list won't be the first (Love is..., the Book of Love, counting the ways)
11. nor the end-all (certainly not in 130 pages or 130 volumes, lifetimes, generations),
12. but I will love (enjoy, be passionate and care about) finding words to fill these pages.

It is a big subject, love, but I can think of no better guide than words hinted to above, at the heart of a letter written two thousand years ago from Paul of Tarsus to the people of Corinth. This passage is what led me to these three books in the first place. "Faith, hope, and love remain, these three," Paul wrote, "and the greatest of these is love."[3]

---

[3] Paul the Apostle, I Corinthians 13:13 (ca. 56, tr. NRSV 2021).

This is the roadmap that Paul has given us:

> Love is patient; love is kind; love is not envious or boastful or arrogant or rude. It does not insist on its own way; it is not irritable; it keeps no record of wrongs; it does not rejoice in wrongdoing, but rejoices in the truth. It bears all things, believes all things, hopes all things, endures all things. Love never ends.[4]

Based on this, here is my legend for the pages ahead:

1. Love is patient. The Time of Love is well-paced, long-suffering and never short-tempered.

2. Love is kind. The Act of Love is merciful, gentle and unimposing.

3. Love is giving. The Gift of Love is charitable, gracious and unenvying.

4. Love is humble. The Selflessness of Love is modest, emptying and never proud.

---

[4] Paul the Apostle, I Corinthians 13:4-8a (ca. 56, tr. NRSV 2021).

5. Love is respectful. The Language of Love is tolerant, self-controlled and conscientious.

6. Love is peaceful. The Contentedness of Love is serene, calm and uninsisting.

7. Love is joyful. The Voice of Love is passionate, rejoicing and truth-celebrating.

8. Love is compassionate. The Care of Love is listening, attending and carrying the weight.

9. Love is faithful. The Commitment of Love is loyal, trustworthy and tomorrow-believing.

10. Love is hopeful. The Affirmation of Love promising, assuring and optimistic.

11. Love is enduring. The Life of Love is strong, bearing and outlasting.

12. Love is eternal. The Forever of Love is steadfast, always and never-ending.

With this, let our journey begin!

Faith, hope, and love remain, these three,
and the greatest of these is love.
— *Paul the Apostle* [5]

---

[5] See page 7.

Facing page: J. Vold, The Many Words of Love (2022).

iii.

The Many Words of Love

Positively, know and learn: love is
patient and kind, rejoicing in truth
and in all things, bearing,
believing, hoping and enduring.

Negatively, love in turn is not
envious, boastful, arrogant or rude,
insistent, irritable, resentful or
finding joy in what is wrong.

Positively, turn it around: love is
giving, selfless, humble, respectful,
tolerant, peaceful, contented and
finding joy again in what is right
and celebrating what is true,

the ultimate double negative to
always remember: love never ends.

Love is all that Paul says it is, but there are many other ways to say it. In Latin, love is amor (affection) and dilectio (delight) but also caritas (charity), the root of the Celtic cara.

In Hebrew, love is ahava but also chesed, which is love extended as a covenant, often translated as mercy or loving kindness.

In eastern religions, love is in the four immeasurables of the Brahmavihara: maitri (loving-kindness or benevolence); karuna (compassion); mudita (empathetic joy) and upeksa (equanimity).[6] Hindus also promote kama (sensual desire) as one of the four goals of a fulfilling life.[7] Spiritual meditation frequently turns to the Hindu maitri (metta in Buddhism), beginning with an inward loving-kindness that is then turned outward.

In deaf communications, International Sign shows love by kissing the back of the fist (being crazy about) or crossing fisted arms over the chest and hugging oneself. American Sign

---

[6] Anon., The Brahma Abodes Suta (ca. 100, as cited by Buddhagosa, The Path of Purification, ca. 500).

[7] Anon., Ramayana and Mahabharata texts (ca. 100).

Language expresses love by an outward fisted palm with extended thumb, index and pinky, combining the signs of I, L and Y (I love you).

The Greeks have nine words for love: agape (unconditional love), philia (attraction), storge (natural affection), pragma (commitment), thelema (willful love), ludus (playful love), xenia (hospitality), eros (desire), and mania (obsession). Plato's dialogues also introduced to the love of Diotima's Ladder, appreciating in six steps the beauty of a particular body, all bodies, souls, laws and institutions (conservatism), knowledge and finally love itself.[8]

According to C. S. Lewis, we can recognize love in categories of gift loves (philia and agape) and need-loves (storge and eros).[9]

According to John Allen Lee there are fifteen colors of love, divided into primary colors (eros, ludus and storge), secondary colors (agape, pragma and mania), and tertiary combinations of these (e.g., manic storge, agapic ludus and pragmatic eros).[10]

---

[8] Plato, Symposium (ca. 370 BC).

[9] C. S. Lewis, Four Loves (1960).

[10] John Allen Lee, Colours of Love (1973).

Merriam-Webster's definition of love is long,[11]

---

[11]

From Merriam-Webster.com (2021): love: [[A]] noun. 1 [[affection or attraction.]]. a: [a feeling of strong or constant affection for a person]. i: strong affection for another arising out of kinship or personal ties. ii: attraction based on sexual desire : affection and tenderness felt by lovers. iii: affection based on admiration, benevolence, or common interests. b: an assurance of affection. 2: warm attachment, enthusiasm, or devotion. 3 [[someone or something that is loved.]]. a: the object of attachment, devotion, or admiration. b: [a person you love in a romantic way]. (1): a beloved person : DARLING —often used as a term of endearment. (2) British —used as an informal term of address. 4 [[unselfish concern or the reaction to this]]. a : unselfish loyal and benevolent (*see BENEVOLENT sense 1a*) concern for the good of another: such as (1): the fatherly concern of God for humankind, (2): brotherly concern for others. b: a person's adoration of God. 5: a god (such as Cupid or Eros) or personification of love. 6: an amorous episode : LOVE AFFAIR. 7: the sexual embrace : COPULATION. 8: a score of zero (as in tennis). 9 *capitalized, Christian Science* : GOD. at love : holding one's opponent scoreless in tennis. in love : inspired by affection. [[B]] verb: transitive. 1: to hold dear : CHERISH. 2 [[to feel affection for]]. a: to feel a lover's passion, devotion, or tenderness for. b [[to act on the feeling of affection]]. (1): CARESS. (2): to fondle amorously. (3): to copulate with. 3: to like or desire actively : take pleasure in. 4: to thrive in. [[C]] intransitive verb: to feel affection or experience desire.

Oxford's definition of love is even longer:[12]

---

[12]

From Oxford University Press, Oxford English and American Dictionaries (2020): Love. I. Senses relating to affection and attachment. 1. a. A feeling or disposition of deep affection or fondness for someone, typically arising from a recognition of attractive qualities, from natural affinity, or from sympathy and manifesting itself in concern for the other's welfare and pleasure in his or her presence (distinguished from sexual love at sense 4a); great liking, strong emotional attachment; (similarly) a feeling or disposition of benevolent attachment experienced towards a group or category of people, and (by extension) towards one's country or another impersonal object of affection. With of, for, to, towards.   b. As an abstract quality or principle. (Sometimes personified.) c. As a count noun: an instance of affection or fondness. Also: an act of kindness (obsolete). d. In Old English (contrasted with lagu law): amicable or peaceable settlement (as opposed to litigation). Hence (in later use) occasionally rendering Latin foedus treaty, covenant. Obsolete.   2. In religious use: the benevolence and affection of God towards an individual or towards creation; (also) the affectionate devotion due to God from an individual; regard and consideration of one human being towards another prompted by a sense of a common relationship to God. Cf. charity n. 1. 3. Strong predilection, liking, or fondness (for something); devotion (to something). With of, for (also †to, †unto); in Old English also with the genitive. 4. a. An intense feeling of romantic attachment based on an attraction felt by one person for another; intense liking and concern for another person, typically combined with sexual passion. Cf. true love n. 1. b. An instance of being in love. Also in plural: love affairs, amatory relations. c. The motif of romantic love in imaginative literature. 5. Sexual desire or lust, esp. as a physiological instinct; amorous sexual activity, sexual intercourse. Cf. to make love at Phrases 3a. 6. a. A person who is beloved of another, esp. a sweetheart (cf. true love n. 4a); also (rare) in extended use of animals. Cf. lady-love n. 1. b. As a form of address to one's beloved and (in modern informal use) also familiarly to a close acquaintance or (more widely) anyone whom one encounters. Frequently with possessive adjective. c. In reference to illicit relations: a paramour or lover (applied to both men and women). Obsolete. d. gen. An object of love; a person who or thing which is loved, the beloved (of); a passion, preoccupation. See also first love n. d. at first adj., adv., and n.2 Compounds 1b(b). e. colloquial. A charming or delightful person or thing. a. Now with capital initial. The personification of romantic or sexual affection, usually portrayed as masculine, and more or less identified with the Eros, Amor, or Cupid of Classical mythology (formerly sometimes feminine, and capable of being identified with Venus). See also Phrases 6b. b. In plural. Representations or personifications of Cupid; mythological gods of love, or attendants of the goddess of love; figures or representations of the god of love. Frequently with modifying word. II. Senses relating to games of skill or chance. 8. A game of chance of Italian origin in which one player holds up a certain number of fingers, and another simultaneously guesses their number; = morra n. Frequently in the play of love. Obsolete. a. In various competitive games of skill, esp. tennis, squash, bridge, and whist: no score, (a score of)

I am forever learning about love: the give and the need; the agape, philios and eros; the ladder and the wheel, the immeasurable virtues of benevolence, compassion, empathy and equanimity and the many ways to express love. I appreciate every definition, every dimension, every word of love, and I hope to keep learning as long as I live. But for this book, I will especially follow Paul's beautiful exposition of agape, giving us characteristics that every love should have, regardless of what the dictionary says, and all of these should go into my love to you: patience, kindness, generosity, humility, respect, peace, joy, compassion, faith, hope, endurance, eternity.

---

nothing, nil. Frequently in various formulaic expressions indicating the score of two contestants in a game (as fifteen love, six love, etc.). 9. Tennis. to love: (with reference to a game) with one player winning no points; (with reference to a set) with one player winning no games. 10. A variant of the game of euchre (euchre n.). Obsolete. III. Other uses. 11. A thin crape or gauze material, formerly worn when in mourning; a border of this. Obsolete. 12. a. Traveller's joy, Clematis vitalba; = love-bind n. at Compounds. Obsolete. 13. Australian. A twining plant, Comesperma volubile (family Polygalaceae), having narrow leaves and masses of bright purple flowers. Also love creeper.

Lift your voice to touch my voice now,
Let our song bring joy to earth.

— *Tracy K. Smith* [13]

---

[13] See pages 81-82.

Facing page: J. Vold, The Poetry of Love (2022).

iv.

The Poetry of Love

Someone else wrote the song
that the singer made his own,
and yet another someone else
    was his muse,
but give credit to the cover,
to the spirit of the lover
and the source of love that makes
    the music news.

Someone sing me a sing,
make me want to sing along,
make me feel like every note
    was meant for me
and I'll sing the song to others
so that they can feel it too
and we'll sing the song
    into eternity.

It is easy to turn to poetry and song to fill out this collection, and I will do so without apology. Love is enhanced through poetry and music, and the best thing about a good poem or song is that it invites one to share it with others and inspires more of the same. In that spirit I am opening each chapter with a few inspired words of my own. I had done something similar with My Hope for You and My Faith in You, but this time I am doing it more appropriately, with poetry sparked by what others have said about love.

This is, in fact, the spirit by which I am sharing all the words that follow, like a singer covering the songs of others. In honor of the love song cover, and to start this collection out with the right mood, I begin with a few lines from some classic love songs, written by one, sung by another and kept alive by many repeaters.

Up first is an extended tribute to a song Peter Gabriel sung in 2004, covering what The Magnetic Fields first sang in 1999, their answer, it would seem, to the Monotones in 1957, who famously crooned: "Oh I wonder, wonder, wonder, oh, who, who, who wrote the book of love?" You did! Or at least you read it and sang it to me, and maybe that's all that matters, even more than the words themselves.

- The book of love is long and boring
No one can lift the damn thing
It's full of charts and facts and figures
And instructions for dancing
But I, I love it when you read to me
And you, you can read me anything.

  The book of love has music in it
In fact that's where music comes from
Some of it is just transcendental
Some of it is just really dumb
But I, I love it when you sing to me
And you, you can sing me anything.
  > *Stephin Merritt, The Book of Love (1999, first sung by Merritt for The Magnetic Fields, later covered by Peter Gabriel, 2004, with eponymous credit to Warren Davis, George Malone and Charles Patrick, The Book of Love, 1957, recorded by The Monotones).*

- Heaven, I'm in heaven, and my heart
beats so that I can hardly speak.
  > *Irving Berlin, Cheek to Cheek (1935, performed by Fred Astaire as Jerry Travers in Top Hat, later covered by Ella Fitzgerald and Louis Armstrong, 1956).*

- I see your face in every flower, your eyes
in stars above.
  > *Ray Noble, The Very Thought of You (1934, first performed by Noble's orchestra with Al Bowlly on vocals, later covered by Billie Holliday 1938).*

- My love must be a kind of blind love, I can't see anyone but you.

  Al Dubin and Harry Warren, I Only Have Eyes For You (1934, performed by Dick Powell as Jimmy Higgins in Dames, later covered by The Flamingos, 1959).

- In other words, hold my hand, in other words, baby, kiss me. ...I love you.

  Bart Howard, In Other Words (Fly Me to the Moon) (1954, originally performed by Felicia Sanders at the Blue Angels Supper Club, first recorded by Kaye Ballard, 1954, then covered by Frank Sinatra 1964).

- If anyone should ever write my life story ...you're the best thing that ever happened to me.

  Jim Weatherly, You're the Best Thing That Ever Happened To Me (1971, first recorded privately by Danny Thomas, Weatherly's manager's father in law, as a gift to his wife, first sung commercially by Ray Price, 1973, later covered by Gladys Knight and the Pips, 1974).

- My lonely days are over and life is like a song.

  Mack Gorden and Harry Warren, At Last (1941, first performed without vocals by the Glenn Miller Orchestra in Sun Valley Serenade, first sung with vocals by Lynn Bari as Jaynie Stevens in Orchestra Wives, 1942, later covered by Etta James, 1960).

- Grow old along with me! The best is yet to be.

    Robert Browning, Rabbi ben Ezra, 1864, a poem quoted in A Love Affair: The Eleanor and Lou Gehrig Story, 1978, inspiring a song by John Lennon and Yoko Ono, ca. 1980, released posthumously in 1984, three years after Lennon's death, later covered by Mary Chapin Carpenter, 1995).

- No, I won't be afraid just as long as you stand by me.

    Stand by Me, Ben E. King, Jerry Lieber and Mike Stoller (1961, later covered by John Lennon, 1975).

- God speed your love to me.

    Alex North and Hy Zaret, Unchained Melody (1954, performed by Todd Duncan as Bill Howard in Unchained, later covered by the Righteous Brothers, 1965).

- It's very clear our love is here to stay.

    George Gershwin and Ira Gershwin, Love Is Here to Stay (1937, performed by Kenny Baker as Danny Beecher in The Goldwyn Follies, 1938, later covered by Gene Kelly, 1951).

- I'm wishing you joy and happiness,
  But above all this, I wish you love.

    Dolly Parton, I Will Always Love You (1973, first sung by Parton, later covered by Whitney Houston on the soundtrack of The Bodyguard, 1992).

For that I have you in my heart.
— *Paul the Apostle* [14]

---

[14] See page 27.

Facing Page: J. Vold, The Heart of Love (2022).

v.

The Heart of Love

With every love,
the lover lives in the beloved
and the beloved lives in the lover

the beloved lives in the lover
by being in the lover's hold
and in the lover's heart

and the lover lives in the beloved
by wanting more than an acquainting hold
and the feeling of a beating heart

the lover wants to know
all there is to know of the beloved
to let the beloved live in the lover's soul.

There is one place we ought to visit before we set out on this journey, a lovely stop, it would seem, at the center of many love songs and the target of Cupid's arrow, and yet it does not seem to be on Paul's roadmap. I am speaking, of course, of the heart, that vital muscle that throbs and aches and sometimes breaks within us. Literally, it is the essence of our being, a part of us that we cannot do without. Metaphorically speaking, the heart is the core of our emotions, a place that can be passionate or lonely, desirous or cold.

Lest metaphors be mixed, the heart is clearly not a stop, but there are places for the heart in our journey ahead. One can be kind-hearted, or have a giving heart or have a heart-felt hope. One's heart can be full of joy, at peace, in love. But the heart is also a stubborn organ that can be selfish more than humble, suffering more than compassionate, possessive more than respectful. In the end, it is brittle more than enduring and not as "forever" as we want it to be.

Do not lose heart, though. I am not asking you to check your hearts at the gate. But remember this: if love is a matter of the heart, it should be about two hearts, or the heart of a community, not the heart of a traveler with no place to go. And if the heart is going to be about love, it will do best if it takes the higher road.

- It is right for me to think this way about all of you, because I hold you in my heart*... [*Translator's footnote: Or because you hold me in your heart].

  Paul the Apostle, Philippians 1:7 (ca. 62, tr. NRSV, 2021).

- Every love makes the beloved to be in the lover, and vice versa...the beloved is said to be in the lover, inasmuch as the beloved abides in the apprehension of the lover, according to Philippians 1:7, "For that I have you in my heart": while the lover is said to be in the beloved, according to apprehension, inasmuch as the lover is not satisfied with a superficial apprehension of the beloved, but strives to gain an intimate knowledge of everything pertaining to the beloved, so as to penetrate into his very soul.

  Thomas Aquinas, Summa Theologica (ca. 1270, tr. Fathers of the English Dominican Province, 1920).

- i carry your heart (i carry it in my heart)...

  e. e. cummings, [i carry your heart with me (i carry it in] (1952).

Love is...
amor, dilectio, caritas, ahava, chesed,
maitri, karuna, mudita, upeksa, kama,
metta, agape, philia, storge, pragma,
thelema, ludus, xenia, eros, mania,
and
patience, kindness, generosity, humility,
respect, peace, joy, compassion, faith,
hope, endurance, eternity.

Reflections of Love

Patience is the guardian of faith, the preserver of peace, the cherisher of love.

— *George Horne* [15]

---

[15] See page 32.

Facing Page: J. Vold, Patience (2022).

1.

Patience

In time love will happen,
and in its own time,
not on time by standards imposed
but over time, and after some time,
taking the time that it needs
to ripen and bloom, to be kissed by the sun,
to be filled with the life of the wind,
to grow, to keep growing and never be done,
to be timeless through harvest and seed.

If time could stand still
like some once upon time
in those stories that everyone knows,
we'd have a good time,
we'd have nothing but time
to live happily ever however it goes,
but in love time will happen,
and all love begins
with patience, the pulse of forever within.

- Patience is the guardian of faith, the preserver of peace, the cherisher of love, the teacher of humility; Patience governs the flesh, strengthens the spirit, sweetens the temper, stifles anger, extinguishes envy, subdues pride; she bridles the tongue, refrains the hand, tramples upon temptations, endures persecutions, consummates martyrdom; Patience produces unity in the church, loyalty in the State, harmony in families and societies; she comforts the poor and moderates the rich; she makes us humble in prosperity, cheerful in adversity, unmoved by calumny and reproach; she teaches us to forgive those who have injured us, and to be the first in asking forgiveness of those whom we have injured; she delights the faithful, and invites the unbelieving; she adorns the woman, and approves the man; is loved in a child, praised in a young man, admired in an old man; she is beautiful in either sex and every age.

  George Horne, Patience Portrayed (1762).

- Patience with others is Love, Patience with self is Hope, Patience with God is Faith.

  Adel Bestavros (ca. 2005; as cited by Tomas Halik, Patience with God, 2009).

- Patience is enduring love; experience is perfecting love; and hope is exulting love.
  Alexander Dickson, Beauty for Ashes (1878).

- Endurance is the crowning quality,
  And patience all the passion of great
      hearts.
  James Russell Lowell, Columbus (1844).

- Remember that time slurs over everything, lets all deeds fade, blurs all writings and kills all memories. Exempt are only those which dig into the hearts of men by love.
  Aristotle, Letter to Alexander on the Policy toward the Cities (ca. 342 BC; as cited by Anon., Arabic transcript, 1891, tr. unknown as cited by Christopher Jackson, Roger Federer: Portrait of an Artist, 2017).

- And is not time even as love is,
      undivided and spaceless?

  But if in you thought you must measure
      time into seasons, let each season
      encircle all the other seasons,

  And let today embrace the past with
      remembrance and the future with
      longing.
  Khalil Gibran, The Prophet (1923).

- Patience is a nobler motion than any deed.

  Cyrus Augustus Bartol, Radical Problems (1872).

- Sometimes when we have been overcome by pride or impatience, and we want to improve our rough and bearish manners, we complain that we require solitude, as if we should find the virtue of patience there where nobody provokes us: and we apologize for our carelessness, and say that the reason of our disturbance does not spring from our own impatience, but from the fault of our brethren. And while we lay the blame of our fault on others, we shall never be able to reach the goal of patience and perfection. The chief part then of our improvement and peace of mind must not be made to depend on another's will, which cannot possibly be subject to our authority, but it lies rather in our own control. And so the fact that we are not angry ought not to result from another's perfection, but from our own virtue, which is acquired, not by somebody else's patience, but by our own long-suffering.

  John Cassian, Institutes of the Coenobia (ca. 420, tr. C. S. Gibson 1894).

- If you have patience, then you'll also have love. Patience leads to love.

  Mata Amritanandamayi, conversation with Riitta Uosukainen (2000, as reported on amritapuri.org).

- Let us apply patience as well, for without patience nothing can be achieved. Verily, very often people give up a brilliant beginning only because of lack of patience.

  Helena Roerich, Letter to America (1931, tr. V. L. Dutko, 1954).

- So like children, we begin again...

  to fall,
  patiently to trust our heaviness.
  Even a bird has to do that
  before he can fly.

  Rainer Maria Rilke, The Book of Hours (1905).

- Seek patience
  and passion
  in equal amounts.

  Patience alone
  will not build the temple.

  Passion alone
  will destroy its walls.

  Maya Angelou, Seek Patience (ca. 2014).

- I have just three things to teach:
      simplicity, patience, compassion.
  These three are your greatest treasures.
  Simple in actions and in thoughts,
      you return to the source of being.
  Patient with both friends and enemies,
      you accord with the way things are.
  Compassionate toward yourself,
      you reconcile all beings in the world.
  > *Laozi, Tao Te Ching (ca. 479 BC, tr. Stephen Mitchell, 1988).*

- We need enlightenment. We need more light about each other. Light creates understanding, understanding creates love, love creates patience, and patience creates unity.
  > *Malcolm X, Letter to the Egyptian Gazette (1964).*

- Clothe yourselves with compassion, kindness, humility, meekness, and patience. ...Above all, clothe yourselves with love, which binds everything together in perfect harmony.
  > *Paul the Apostle, Colossians 3: 12-14 (ca. 62, tr. NRSV, 2021).*

- Love is patient...
  > *Paul the Apostle, 1 Corinthians 1:3 (ca. 56, tr. NRSV, 2021).*

My love to you... is a meal carefully prepared, tendered with time and seasoned to perfection; and when served it is a moment to share and savor, well worth the wait and not to be rushed.

Love all these things which are about to
leave. The rocks are watching, and the
squirrels and the stars and the tired
people in the street.
If you love them, let them know.
— *Anne Herbert* [16]

---

[16] See page 40.

Facing Page: J. Vold, Kindness (2022).

2.

Kindness

Love is patient with all things that are about
to leave.
Love is kind with random acts of senseless
beauty.
Love is generous with grace and
non-invasive extravagance.
Love is humble. The rocks are watching, and
the squirrels.
Love is respectful, letting loved ones know
they are loved.
Love is peaceful, seen by the stars and the
tired people in the street.
Love is joyful; it colors outside the lines.
Love is caring in gorgeous and surprising
ways.
Love is faithful to all that it cares about.
Love is hopeful that all may endure.
Love is enduring with practice over time.
Love is eternal, the last chance to continue.

- Love all these things which are about to leave. The rocks are watching, and the squirrels and the stars and the tired people in the street. If you love them, let them know, with grace and non-invasive extravagance. Care about the beings you care about in gorgeous and surprising ways. Color outside the lines. Practice random kindness and senseless acts of beauty. This is your last chance.

   Anne Herbert, Handy tips on how to behave at the death of the world (Whole Earth Review, Spring 1995).

- Anything you want there to be more of, do it randomly. It will make itself be more, senselesssly. Scrawl it on the wall: RANDOM KINDNESS AND SENSELESS ACTS OF BEAUTY.

   Anne Herbert, Random kindness senseless acts of beauty (Whole Earth Review, July 1985).

- On that best portion of a good man's life,
   His little, nameless, unremembered acts
   Of kindness and of love.

   William Wordsworth, Lines Composed Above Tintern Abbey (1798).

- Let grace and goodness be the principal lodestone of thy affections. For love which hath ends, will have an end; whereas that which is founded on true virtue, will always continue.

  Thomas Fuller, The Holy State and the Profane State (1642)

- This is my simple religion. There is no need for temples; no need for complicated philosophy. Our own brain, our own heart is our temple; the philosophy is kindness.

  Dalai Lama XIV, A Policy of Kindness (1990).

- Goodwill is man's first attempt to express the love of God. Its results on earth will be peace. It is so simple and practical that people fail to appreciate its potency or its scientific and dynamic effect. One person sincerely practising goodwill in a family, can completely change its attitudes. Goodwill really practised among groups in any nation, by political and religious parties in any nation, and among the nations of the world, can revolutionise the world.

  Alice Bailey, Problems Of Humanity (1944).

- Let none deceive another, or despise any being in any state. Let none through anger or ill-will wish harm upon another. Even as a mother protects with her life her child, her only child, so with a boundless heart should one cherish all living beings, radiating kindness over the entire world spreading upwards to the skies and downwards to the depths; outwards and unbounded, freed from hatred and ill-will. Whether standing or walking, seated or lying down, free from drowsiness, one should sustain this recollection. This is said to be the sublime abiding.

  Gautama Buddha, Pali Metta Sutta (ca. 400 BC; as cited by Amaravati Sangha, The Buddha's Teaching on Loving-kindness, 2004).

- To see with the eyes of the heart; to hear the roar of the world with the ears of the heart; to peer into the future with the understanding of the heart; to remember past accumulations through the heart—that is how the aspirant must boldly advance on the path of ascent.

  Helena Roerich and Nicolas Roerich, Agni Yoga, Heart (1932).

- The relationship between men and women should, and can be, characterized not by patronizing behavior or exploitation, but by *metta* (that is to say loving kindness), partnership and trust.
  Aung San Suu Kyi, Opening Keynote Address at NGO Forum on Women, Beijing China (1995).

- I expect to pass through this world but once. Any good, therefore, that I can do or any kindness I can show to any fellow creature, let me do it now. Let me not defer or neglect it for I shall not pass this way again.
  Stephen Grellet (ca. 1855; as cited by W, Gurney Benham, Book of Quotations, Proverbs and Household Words, 1907).

- Wherever there is a human being there is an opportunity for a kindness.
  Seneca the Younger, De Vita Beata (ca. 58, tr. John W, Basore, 1932).

- Just because an animal is large, it doesn't mean he doesn't want kindness; however big Tigger seems to be, remember that he wants as much kindness as Roo.
  A. A. Milne, The House at Pooh Corner (1928).

- come on sweetheart
  let's adore one another
  before there is no more
  of you and me

  a mirror tells the truth
  look at your grim face
  brighten up and cast away
  your bitter smile

  a generous friend
  gives life for a friend
  let's rise above this
  animalistic behavior
  and be kind to one another
  > *Rumi, Ghazal 1535 (ca. 1273), tr. Nader Khalili, Rumi: Fountain of Fire 1994).*

- Let no one ever come to you without leaving better and happier. Be the living expression of God's kindness: kindness in your face, kindness in your eyes, kindness in your smile.
  > *Mother Teresa (ca. 1997; as cited by John Templeton, Worldwide Laws of Life, 1998).*

- And then she asks me, "Do you feel alright?"
  And I say, "Yes, I feel wonderful tonight."
  > *Eric Clapton, Wonderful Tonight (1977).*

My love to you... is a mirror of goodness captured and redirected to you, giving you light to help you through, sometimes shining your own light back to you.

It's all I have to bring today—
This, and my heart beside
    — Emily Dickinson [17]

---

[17] See page 48.

Facing Page: J. Vold, Giving (2022).

3.

Giving

These songs I sing to you were never mine
to claim, just as the love I have for you
cannot be mine to keep. What's journeyed through
     through
my heart and soul, each note of every line,
I've tried to make my own to give to you
but I'm not author of this book I sign
and whatever I give, the rose, the wine,
the words, the song and every dream come true
     true,
precedes my giving. Such is the design
of love: I cannot be composer of
the ground beneath your feet nor sky above,
but I can give you everything that's mine
to give, all I've been given from the start:
the hope of dreams, the faith in what is true,
the journey and the urge to sing to you,
the fire and the beating of my heart.

- It's all I have to bring today —
  This, and my heart beside —
  This, and my heart, and all the fields —
  And all the meadows wide —
  Be sure you count — should I forget
  Some one the sum could tell —
  This, and my heart, and all the Bees
  Which in the Clover dwell.
  > *Emily Dickinson, It's All I Have to Bring Today (1896).*

- I give thee all — I can no more
  Though poor the off'ring be;
  My heart and lute are all the store
  That I can bring to thee.
  A lute whose gentle song reveals
  The soul of love full well;
  And, better far, a heart that feels
  Much more than lute could tell.
  > *Thomas Moore, My Heart and Lute (1828).*

- In the heavens there is a sharing of all with each and of each with all. Such sharing goes forth from the two loves of heaven, which are, as has been said, love to the Lord and love towards the neighbor; and to share their delights is the very nature of these loves.
  > *Emanuel Swedenborg, Heaven and Hell (1758, tr. John Ager, 1900).*

- Give with a heart glowing with generous sentiments; give as the fountain gives out its waters from its own swelling depths; give as the air gives its vital breezes, unrestrained and free; give as the sun gives out its light, from the infinite abysses of its own nature.

  David Thomas, The Poor-Laws of the Bible (1861).

- Each of you must give as you have made up your mind, not reluctantly or under compulsion, for God loves a cheerful giver.

  Paul the Apostle, 2 Corinthians 9:7 (ca. 56, tr. NRSV, 2021).

- Charity, by which God and neighbor are loved, is the most perfect friendship.

  Thomas Aquinas, On Charity (ca. 1274, tr. Lottie H. Kendzierski, 1960).

- Charity is universal benevolence, and benevolence is the habit of loving. Moreover to love is to take delight in the happiness of another, or, what amounts to the same thing, it is to regard another's happiness as one's own.

  Gottfried Wilhelm Leibniz, Preface to Codex Juris Gentium Diplomaticus (1693).

- "Faith, hope, and charity, these three; but the greatest of these is charity." There is a deeper meaning in this text than we at first see. Of "these three," two concern ourselves; the third concerns others. When faith and hope fail, as they do sometimes, we must try charity, which is love in action. We must speculate no more on our duty, but simply do it.

  Dinah Craik, Christian's Mistake (1865, citing Paul the Apostle, 1 Corinthians 13:13 (ca. 54, tr. KJV, 1611).

- Beneficence is a duty: he who is often engaged in the discharge of this duty, and beholds the success of his beneficent designs, comes in the end to love him whom he has benefited. When, therefore, it is said, Thou shalt love thy neighbour as thyself, that is not to be understood, thou shalt first love thy neighbour, and then, by means of this love, act kindly towards him; but, contrariwise, do good to thy fellow-men, and this beneficence will work in thee philanthropy, i.e., a habitude or inclination to be beneficent.

  Immanuel Kant, The Metaphysics of Ethics (1780, tr. J. W. Semple, 1886).

- Thousands of candles can be lit from a
  single candle,
  And the life of the candle will not be
  shortened.
  Happiness never decreases by being
  shared.
  > *Bukkyo Dendo Kyokai, The Teachings of*
  > *Buddha (1972)*

- Take my hand, take my whole life, too.
  > *George David Weiss, Luigi Creatore and*
  > *Hugo Peretti, Can't Help Falling in Love*
  > *With You (1961, recorded by Elvis Presley).*

- There's a river born to be a giver
  Keep you warm won't let you shiver
  His heart isn't ever gonna wither
  Come on everybody time to deliver

  Give it away give it away
    give it away now...
  > *John Anthony Frusciante, Michael Peter*
  > *Balzary, Give it Away (1989, Red Hot Chili*
  > *Peppers).*

- One river gives its journey to the next.
  > *Alberto Rios, Epigraph to When Giving Is All*
  > *We Have (2014).*

• We give because someone gave to us.
We give because nobody gave to us.

We give because giving has changed us.
We give because giving could have
    changed us.

We have been better for it,
We have been wounded by it—

Giving has many faces: It is loud and
    quiet,
Big, though small, diamond in
    wood-nails.

Its story is old, the plot worn and the
    pages too,
But we read this book, anyway, over
    and again:

Giving is, first and every time, hand to
    hand,
Mine to yours, yours to mine.

You gave me blue and I gave you
    yellow.
Together we are simple green. You gave
    me

What you did not have, and I gave you
What I had to give—together, we made

Something greater from the difference.
    Alberto Rios, When Giving Is All We Have
    (2014).

My love to you... is what I give to you: the appreciation of your presence and the active gratitude that we are not alone. The more I am aware of you, the more I want to give.

*Selflessness is my true self. Love is my
true character. Love is my name.*

— *Thomas Merton* [18]

---

[18] See page 56.

Facing Page: Humility (2022).

4.

Humility

Somehow,
patiently biding time,
kindly becoming aware,
generously giving away,
humbly making amends,
respectfully shaking hands,
peacefully sharing a smile,
joyfully singing out loud,
mercifully bearing the load,
faithfully remaining true,
hopefully looking beyond,
enduringly living in love,
eternally staying alive,
the self becomes
selfless.

- To say that I am made in the image of God is to say that Love is the reason for my existence, for God is love. Love is my true identity. Selflessness is my true self. Love is my true character. Love is my name.
  Thomas Merton, Seeds of Contemplation (1949).

- Humility is not thinking less of yourself, but thinking of yourself less. Humility is thinking more of others.
  Rick Warren, The Purpose-Driven Life (2002).

- There is, therefore, something in humility which, strangely enough, exalts the heart.
  Augustine of Hippo, City of God (ca. 420, tr. Marcus Dods, 1871).

- When I give I give myself.
  Walt Whitman, Song of Myself (1855).

- I can't tell one from another:
  Did I find you, or you find me?
  Chris Frantz, Tina Weymouth, David Byrne and Jerry Harrison, This Must Be The Place (Naive Melody), (1983, Talking Heads).

- From each a mystic silence Love
     demands.
  What do all seek so earnestly?
     'Tis Love.
  What do they whisper to each other?
     Love.
  Love is the subject of their inmost
     thoughts.
  In Love, no longer "thou" and "I" exist,
  For Self has passed away in the Beloved.
  > *Anon., Jawhar al-dāt (ca. 1335, tr. Margaret Smith, Intoxicated by the Wine of Love, 1932).*

- Love is the perception of individuals. Love is the extremely difficult realisation that something other than oneself is real. Love, and so art and morals, is the discovery of reality.
  > *Iris Murdoch, The Sublime and the Good (1959).*

- The genuinely humble look not at the outcome of their humility. True humility does not know that it is humble. If it did, it would be proud from the contemplation of so fine a virtue.
  > *Martin Luther, Christmas Sermon (ca. 1546, tr. Roland H. Baintin, 1948).*

- If then there is any comfort in Christ, any consolation from love, any partnership in the Spirit, any tender affection and sympathy, make my joy complete: be of the same mind, having the same love, being in full accord and of one mind. Do nothing from selfish ambition or empty conceit, but in humility regard others as better than yourselves. Let each of you look not to your own interests, but to the interests of others.

  Paul the Apostle, Philippians 2:1-3 (ca. 62, tr. NRSV, 2021).

- What does the Lord require of you but to do justice, and to love kindness, and to walk humbly with your God?

  Micah, Micah 6:8 (ca. 696 BC, tr. NRSV, 2021).

- Humbly I adore thee,
    Verity unseen,
  Who thy glory hidest
    'neath these shadows mean;
  Lo, to thee surrendered,
    my whole heart is bowed,
  Tranced as it beholds thee,
    shrined within the cloud.

  Thomas Aquinas, Adoro Te Devote (1264, tr. Gerald Manley Hopkins, one of several Hopkins versions, ca. 1889).

- Small service is true service while it lasts:
Of humblest friends, bright Creature!
 scorn not one;
The Daisy, by the shadow that it casts,
Protects the lingering dew drop from
 the Sun.
  *William Wordsworth, To a Child (1934,
  written in the album of his god-daughter
  Rotha Quillinan).*

- Sometimes in life we are called to do great things. But as a saint of our times has said, every day we are called to do small things with great love. The most important tasks of a democracy are done by everyone.
  *George W. Bush, First Inaugural Address
  (2001).*

- We can do no great things, only small things with great love.
  *Mother Teresa (ca. 1997, but refuted by
  Mother Teresa Center, San Ysidro, CA,
  2010).*

- God has created us so we do small things with great love.
  *Mother Teresa (ca. 1996, as cited by José Luis
  González-Balado, Mother Teresa: In Her Own
  Words, 1996).*

- True Love is but a humble, low-born thing.
  James Russell Lowell, Love (1840).

- Whoever wishes to become great among you must be your servant.
  > *Jesus (ca. 33; as cited by Anon., Mark 10:43, ca. 74, tr. NRSV, 2021).*

- Everybody can be great, because everybody can serve. You don't have to have a college degree to serve. You don't have to make your subject and your verb agree to serve. You don't have to know about Plato and Aristotle to serve. You don't have to know Einstein's theory of relativity to serve. You don't have to know the second theory of thermodynamics in physics to serve. You only need a heart full of grace, a soul generated by love.
  > *Martin Luther King Jr., The Drum Major Instinct (1968, adapted from sermon by J. Wallace Hamilton, Drum-Major Instincts, 1949).*

- Of every noble work the silent part is
    best,
  Of all expression that which can not be
    expressed.
  > *William Wetmore Story, The Unexpressed (1886).*

- Even when it speaks, humility listens.
  > *Thomas Merton, Thoughts in Solitude (1958).*

My love to you... takes the best selfies of us: it focuses on you without my thumb in the way, stands by you without casting a shadow and cherishes the moment because you are in it.

If I speak in the tongues of mortals and of angels, but do not have love, I am a noisy gong or a clanging cymbal.

— Paul the Apostle [19]

---

[19] See page 64.

Facing Page: J. Vold, Respect (2022).

5.

Respect

When I was a child, I thought I knew it all;
speaking in tongues of mortals and angels,
I knew every answer, every solution.

As a child I said I could do it all
with noisy gongs and clanging cymbals;
in childish ways I was moving mountains.

I was loved as a child, or I knew of love,
but I didn't know what to do with love.
I thought it was all about me but I was wrong.
And then I thought I was nothing: wrong again.

A child is a beginning and where to begin,
learning how to understand and what to know,
and a child who is loved, or knows of love,
will begin to love, and in love will grow.

- If I speak in the tongues of humans and of angels but do not have love, I am a noisy gong or a clanging cymbal. And if I have prophetic powers and understand all mysteries and all knowledge and if I have all faith so as to remove mountains but do not have love, I am nothing. ...Love is not envious or boastful or arrogant or rude. It does not insist on its own way; it is not irritable; it keeps no record of wrongs. ....When I was a child, I spoke like a child, I thought like a child, I reasoned like a child. When I became an adult, I put an end to childish ways.

  Paul the Apostle, 1 Corinthians 13:1-2, 4b-5, 11 (ca. 56, tr. NRSV 2021).

- *CLAUDIO*
  Friendship is constant in all other
      things,
  Save in the office and affairs of love:
  Therefore, all hearts in love use their
      own tongues;
  Let every eye negotiate for itself,
  And trust no agent.

  William Shakespeare, Much Ado About Nothing, Act II, Scene 1 (1599).

- The Five Love Languages:
    1. Words of Affirmation
    2. Acts of Service
    3. Gifts
    4. Quality Time
    5. Physical Touch

    ...Love can be expressed and received in all five languages. However, if you don't speak a person's primary love language, that person will not feel loved, even though you may be speaking the other four.

    Gary Chapman, The Five Love Languages: How to Express Heartfelt Commitment to Your Mate (1992).

- To truly love we must learn to mix various ingredients - care, affection, recognition, respect, commitment, and trust, as well as honest and open communication.

    bell hooks, All About Love (2001).

- Happiness abounds when there is genuine respect one for another. Wives draw closer to their husbands, and husbands are more appreciative of their wives, and children are happy, as children are meant to be.

    Thomas S. Monson, An Example of the Believers (1992).

- Love one another, but make not a bond
    of love:
  Let it rather be a moving sea between
    the shores of your souls.
  Fill each other's cup, but drink not from
    one cup.
  Give one another of your bread, but eat
    not from the same loaf.
  Sing and dance together and be joyous,
    but let each of you be alone,
  Even as the strings of a lute are alone
    though they quiver with the same
    music.
  Give your hearts, but not into each
    other's keeping.
  For only the hand of Life can contain
    your hearts.
  And stand together yet not too near
    together:
  For the pillars of the temple stand apart,
  And the oak tree and the cypress grow
    not in each other's shadow.
  Khalil Gibran, The Prophet (1923).

- Ye are the fruits of one tree, and the
  leaves of one branch. Deal ye one with
  another in the utmost love and harmony.
  *Bahá'u'lláh (ca. 1892; as cited by Shoghi
  Effendi, 1935).*

- Respect is not fear and awe; it denotes, in accordance with the root of the word (*respicere* = to look at), the ability to see a person as he is, to be aware of his individuality and uniqueness.
  Erich Fromm, Man for Himself (1947).

- The word "respect" is derived from the Latin *respicere*, which means "to look back at" or "to look again." ...We are called "to look again, and again" at ourselves and others with new eyes, eyes filled with love, compassion, mercy, and forgiveness.
  Jeanne Connolly, Living the Way of Love (2019).

- Occasionally in life there are those moments of unutterable fulfillment which cannot be completely explained by those symbols called words. Their meanings can only be articulated by the inaudible language of the heart.
  Martin Luther King Jr., Nobel acceptance speech (1964).

- Many languages fly around the world producing sparks when they collide sometimes of hate sometimes of love
  Bei Dao, Language (1988, tr. Bonnie S. McDougall, 1990)

- Love is the expansion of two natures in such fashion that each includes the other, each is enriched by the other. Love is an echo in the feelings of a unity subsisting between two persons which is founded both on likeness and on complementary differences.

  Felix Adler, Life and Destiny (1913).

- I see friends shaking hands
  Saying, "How do you do?"
  They're really saying
  "I love you."

  George David Weiss and Bob Thiele, What a Wonderful World (1967, sung by Louis Armstrong).

- Respect is one of the greatest expressions of love. If other people try to write your story, it means they don't respect you. They consider that you're not a good artist who can write your own story, even though you were born to write your own story.

  Miguel Ángel Ruiz, The Fifth Agreement : A Practical Guide to Self-Mastery (2009).

- And you can tell everybody
  This is your song.

  Elton John, Bernie Taupin, Carole Bayer Sager, David W. Foster, Your Song (1970).

My love to you... is yours to begin with, always for you and ultimately yours to cherish. I am happy to tell this story and sing your song, but let me listen too.

*This is what should be done by one who
is skilled in goodness and who knows the
path of peace...*
— Gautama Buddha. [20]

---

[20] See Page 72.

Facing Page: J. Vold, Peace (2022).

6.

Peace

This is what should be wished by those
who know the good and seek the peace:
"In gladness and in safety, may
all living beings be at ease,
whoever they are, omitting none,
whatever they seem, the weak, the strong,

the great and mighty, the short and small,
the all and everyone in between,
those who are seen and those unseen,
those living near, those far away,
those born and those who are yet to be
may each living being be at ease!"

This is what should be wished by those
who know the good and seek the peace,
who know the good and seek the peace,
who know the good and seek the peace...

- This is what should be done by one who is skilled in goodness and who knows the path of peace: Let them be able and upright, straightforward and gentle in speech, humble and not conceited, contented and easily satisfied, unburdened with duties and frugal in their ways. Peaceful and calm, and wise and skillful, not proud and demanding in nature, let them not do the slightest thing that the wise would later reprove, wishing: "In gladness and in safety, may all beings be at ease. Whatever living beings there may be; whether they are weak or strong, omitting none, the great or the mighty, medium, short or small, the seen and the unseen, those living near and far away, those born and to-be-born, may all beings be at ease!"

  Gautama Buddha, Pali Metta Sutta (ca. 400 BC, tr. Amaravati Sangha, The Buddha's Teaching on Loving-kindness, 2004).

- Remember love. The only hope for any of us is peace. ...Get out there and get peace. Think peace, live peace, and breathe peace and you'll get it as soon as you like.

  John Lennon, press statement (1969, as cited by David Pritchard and Alan Lysaght, The Beatles : An Oral History, 1998).

- After love comes peace. I have remarked before, a great many people are trying to make peace. But that has already been done. God has not left it for us to do; all that we have to do is to enter into it. It is a condition, and instead of our trying to make peace and work for peace, we want to cease all that, and sweetly enter into peace.

    Dwight L. Moody, Secret Power (1881).

- There is no way to peace; peace is the way.

    A. J. Muste (ca. 1967, as cited by New York Times, 1967).

- But there is another way. And that is to organize mass non-violent resistance based on the principle of love. It seems to me that this is the only way as our eyes look to the future. As we look out across the years and across the generations, let us develop and move right here. We must discover the power of love, the power, the redemptive power of love. And when we discover that we will be able to make of this old world a new world. We will be able to make men better. Love is the only way.

    Martin Luther King Jr., Loving Your Enemies (November 1957).

- When the Power Of Love will replace the Love Of Power, then will our world know the blessings of Peace.

  William Gladstone (ca 1898, as cited by The National Elementary Principal, 1948).

- The power of love is a curious thing
  Make a one man weep, make another
     man sing
  Change a hawk to a little white dove
  More than a feeling that's the power of
     love.

  Huey Lewis, Chris Hayes, Johnny Colla, The Power of Love (1985).

- If you want to make peace, you don't talk to your friends. You talk to your enemies.

  Moshe Dyan, as quoted in Newsweek (1977).

- If you want to make peace with your enemy, you have to work with your enemy. Then he becomes your partner.

  Nelson Mandela, Long Walk to Freedom (1995).

- Peace is not something you wish for; it's something you make, something you do, something you are, and something you give away!"

  Robert Fulghum, All I Really Need to Know I Learned In Kindergarten (1986).

- Peace will come wherever it is sincerely invited. Love will overflow every sanctuary given it. Truth will grow where the fertilizer that nourishes it is also truth. Faith will be its own reward.
  Alice Walker, The Universe Responds: Or, How I Learned We Can Have Peace on Earth (1989).

- The peace we seek in the world begins in human hearts. And it finds its glorious expression when we look beyond any differences in religion or tribe, and rejoice in the beauty of every soul.
  Barack Obama, Address to the People of India (2015).

- love is a place
  & through this place of
  love move
  (with brightness of peace)
  all places

  yes is a world
  & in this world of
  yes live
  (skilfully curled)
  all worlds
  e. e. cummings, love is a place (1935).

- When it is peace, then we may view again
  With new-won eyes each other's truer
    form
  And wonder. Grown more loving-kind
    and warm
  We'll grasp firm hands and laugh at the
    old pain
  When it is peace. But until peace, the
    storm,
  The darkness and the thunder and the
    rain.
  Charles Sorley, To Germany (ca. 1915).

- Even if there was a gun in my hand and he was standing in front of me, I would not shoot him. This is the compassion I have learned from Mohamed, the prophet of mercy, Jesus Christ and Lord Buddha. This the legacy of change I have inherited from Martin Luther King, Nelson Mandela and Mohammed Ali Jinnah. This is the philosophy of nonviolence that I have learned from Gandhi, Bacha Khan and Mother Teresa. And this is the forgiveness that I have learned from my father and from my mother. This is what my soul is telling me: be peaceful and love everyone.
  Malala Yousafzai , UN Speech (2013).

My love to you... begins with a peace of my heart when I am with you; our love is nurtured by a peace between us as we proceed; and love, if we do it right, expands around us and through us to become a peace of the world.

The fruit of the Spirit is love, joy, peace, patience, kindness, generosity, faithfulness, gentleness, and self-control.

— *Paul the Apostle* [21]

---

[21] See page 80.

Facing Page: J. Vold, Joy (2022).

7.

Joy

Rejoice! In love we can be true
    to one another, and to who
    we are together: love with joy,

patience, kindness, self-control,
    a peaceful mind, a gentle hold,
    a generous heart, a faithful soul.

Rejoice! Love is the first fruit of
    our spirit, and the greatest of
    all that abides within us, ever

bigger than our lasting hope,
    more than the living faith we keep
    is love, outlasting, everliving

love. Rejoice! Give love its voice!
    Let every mind and heart and soul
      rejoice!

- The fruit of the Spirit is love, joy, peace, patience, kindness, generosity, faithfulness, gentleness, and self-control.
  Paul the Apostle, Galatians 5:22-23a (ca. 48, tr. NRSV, 2021).

- Love is the ultimate meaning of everything around us. It is not a mere sentiment; it is truth; it is the joy that is at the root of all creation.
  Rabindranath Tagore, Sādhanā: The Realization of Life (1913).

- Joy! Joy! I triumph! Now no more I know
  Myself as simply me. I burn with love
  Unto myself, and bury me in love.
  Attar of Nishapur, Jawhar al-dhat (ca. 1221, tr. Robert Alfred Vaughan, Hours with the Mystics, 1856).

- There may be Peace without Joy, and Joy without Peace, but the two combined make Happiness.
  John Buchan, Pilgrim's Way (1940).

- I have somewhere surely lived a life of joy with you…
  Walt Whitman, To a Stranger (1860).

- Ask not of me, love, what is love?
  Ask what is good of God above;
  Ask of the great sun what is light;
  Ask what is darkness of the night;
  Ask sin of what may be forgiven;
  Ask what is happiness of heaven;
  Ask what is folly of the crowd;
  Ask what is fashion of the shroud;
  Ask what is sweetness of thy kiss;
  Ask of thyself what beauty is.
  > *Philip James Bailey, Festus: A Party and Entertainment (1813).*

- Love is a great beautifier.
  > *Louisa May Alcott, Little Women (1868).*

- If you've loved another's beauty
  If you've craved the warmth of flesh,
  If your spirit is invested
  In another's sense of worth,
  Lift your voice to touch my voice now,
  Let our song bring joy to earth.
  Lift your voice to touch my voice now,
  Let our song bring joy to earth.

  ...Let us feel it, let us heed it,
  Let us seek its deepest kiss.
  Let us live our brief lives mining
  That which joy alone can give.
  > *Tracy K. Smith, Ode to Joy (2020, adapted from Friedrich Schiller, Ode to Joy, 1785).*

- Who the noble prize achieveth,
  Good friend of a friend to be;
  Who a lovely wife attaineth,
  Join us in his jubilee!
  Yes—he too who but one being
  On this earth can call his own!

  ...Be embrac'd, ye millions yonder!
  Take this kiss throughout the world!
  > *Friedrich Schiller, Ode to Joy (1785, set to music by Ludwig von Beethoven, Symphony No. 9, 1824; tr. William F. Wertz, 1985).*

- Joyful, joyful, we adore Thee,
  God of glory, Lord of love;
  Hearts unfold like flow'rs before Thee,
  Op'ning to the sun above
  > *Henry van Dyke, Hymn of Joy (1907, written to the tune of Ludwig von Beethoven, Symphony No. 9, 1824).*

- My lips will shout for joy when I sing praises to you.
  > *Anon., Psalm 71:23 (ca. 500 BC, tr. NRSV, 2021).*

- When you arise in the morning, think of what a precious privilege it is to be alive – to breathe, to think, to enjoy, to love.
  > *Marcus Aurelius (ca. 180, as cited by Josiah Hotchkiss Gilbert, Dictionary of Burning Words of Brilliant Writers, 1895).*

- I've got that joy, joy , joy, joy
  down in my heart (where?),
  down in my heart to stay.
  George W. Cooke, Joy in My Heart (1925).

- This is what love is. Love is not breathlessness, it is not excitement, it is not the desire to mate every second of the day. It is not lying awake at night imagining that he is kissing every part of your body. No ... don't blush. I am telling you some truths. For that is just being in love; which any of us can convince ourselves we are. Love itself is what is left over, when being in love has burned away. Doesn't sound very exciting, does it? But it is!
  Louis de Bernières, Captain Corelli's Mandolin (1994).

- Joy is not the same as pleasure or happiness. ...Pleasure generally comes from things, and always through the senses; happiness comes from humans through fellowship. Joy comes from loving God and neighbor. Pleasure is quick and violent, like a flash of lightning. Joy is steady and abiding, like a fixed star.
  Fulton J. Sheen, Guide to Contentment (1967).

- Who is the happiest of men? He who
  values the merits of others,
  And in their pleasure takes joy, even as
  though 'twere his own.
    *Johann Wolfgang von Goethe, Distichs
    (ca.1832, tr. Edgar Alfred Bowring, 1853).*

- I love you without knowing how, or
  when, or from where,
  I love you simply, without problems or
  pride:
  I love you in this way because I don't
  know any other way of loving

  but this, in which there is no I or you,
  so intimate that your hand upon my
  chest is my hand,
  so intimate that when I fall asleep it is
  your eyes that close.
    *Pablo Neruda, One Hundred Love Sonnets,
    XVII (1959, tr, Stephen Tapscott, 1986).*

- Love is the magician, the enchanter, that
  changes worthless things to Joy, and
  makes royal kings and queens of common
  clay. It is the perfume of that wondrous
  flower, the heart, and without that sacred
  passion, that divine swoon, we are less
  than beasts; but with it, earth is heaven,
  and we are gods.
    Robert G. Ingersoll, Orthodoxy (1884).

My love to you... is a poem, a song, a shout for joy! Love abides with peace, patience, kindness, generosity, faithfulness, gentleness, and self-control, but love has its voice with joy.

*Simon son of John, do you love me
more than these?*

— *Jesus* [22]

---

[22] See page 88.

Facing Page: J. Vold, Compassion (2022).

8.

Compassion

Agape? asked Jesus to Simon Peter, son of John. Do you love me more than these, but he doesn't say who. More than Simon 's love for others? With more love than others do? Phileo, Peter answered. Lord, you know that I do. Feed my lambs, Jesus told him, but he wasn't quite done.

Agape? asked Jesus to Simon son of John, the same question repeated, but he doesn't qualify. Phileo, Peter said again; he doesn't seem to wonder why. Tend my sheep, Jesus said: another three word reply but with the slightest difference in meaning and tone.

Phileo? asked Jesus to Simon son of John a third time, but now with the disciple's own word, and Simon, rock in Hebrew, Peter, rock in Greek, was hurt. Phileo, Pete sighed. You know everything my Lord. Feed my sheep, Jesus told him, and then he went on.....

- When they had finished breakfast, Jesus said to Simon Peter, "Simon son of John, do you love (agape) me more than these?" He said to him, "Yes, Lord; you know that I love (phileo) you." Jesus said to him, "Feed my lambs." A second time he said to him, "Simon son of John, do you love (agape) me?" He said to him, "Yes, Lord; you know that I love (phileo) you." Jesus said to him, "Tend my sheep." He said to him the third time, "Simon son of John, do you love (phileo) me?" Peter felt hurt because he said to him the third time, "Do you love (phileo) me?" And he said to him, "Lord, you know everything; you know that I love (phileo) you." Jesus said to him, "Feed my sheep."

  Jesus with Peter (ca. 33; as cited by Anon., John 21:15-17 (ca. 100, tr. NRSV, 2021).

- No one has greater love than this, to lay down one's life for one's friends.

  Jesus (ca. 33; a cited by Anon.,, John 15:13, ca. 100, tr. NRSV, 2021).

- You have heard that it was said, 'You shall love (agape) your neighbor and hate your enemy.' But I say to you, Love (agape) your enemies and pray for those who persecute you.

  Jesus (ca. 33; as cited by Anon., Matthew 5:43-44, ca. 95, tr. NRSV, 2021).

- Little children, let us love (agape) not in word or speech, but in deed and truth.

  John the Evangelist, 1 John 3:18 (ca. 100, as cited by Anon., ca. 110, tr. NRSV, 2021).

- Agape means understanding, redeeming good will for all men. It is an overflowing love which is purely spontaneous, unmotivated, groundless, and creative. It is not set in motion by any quality or function of its object... Agape is disinterested love. It is a love in which the individual seeks not his own good, but the good of his neighbor. Agape does not begin by discriminating between worthy and unworthy people, or any qualities people possess. It begins by loving others for their sakes. It is an entirely "neighbor-regarding concern for others," which discovers the neighbor in every man it meets. Therefore, agape makes no distinction between friends and enemy; it is directed toward both. ...Agape is not a weak, passive love. It is love in action... Agape is a willingness to go to any length to restore community... It is a willingness to forgive, not seven times, but seventy times seven to restore community.

  Martin Luther King Jr., An Experiment in Love (1958).

- They also found in combat the closest brotherhood they ever knew. They found selflessness. They found they could love the other guy in their foxhole more than themselves. They found that in war, men who loved life would give their lives for them.

  Stephen Ambrose, Band of Brothers (1992).

- Our job is to love others without stopping to inquire whether or not they are worthy. That is not our business and, in fact, it is nobody's business. What we are asked to do is to love, and this love itself will render both ourselves and our neighbors worthy if anything can. Indeed, that is one of the most significant things about the power of love.

  Thomas Merton, Disputed Questions: The Power and Meaning of Love (1960).

- Agape's object is always the concrete individual, not some abstraction called humanity. Love of humanity is easy because humanity does not surprise you with inconvenient demands. You never find humanity on your doorstep, stinking and begging.

  Peter Kreeft, Fundamentals of the Faith: Essays in Christian Apologetics (1988).

- Agape has nothing to do with the kind of love that depends on the recognition of a valuable quality in its object. Agape does not recognize value, but creates it. Agape loves, and imparts value by loving. The man who is loved by God has no value in himself; what gives him value is precisely the fact that God loves him. Agape is a value-creating principle.

  Anders Nygren, Agape and Eros (1930, tr. P. S. Watson, 1932).

- There is no safe investment. To love at all is to be vulnerable. Love anything, and your heart will certainly be wrung and possibly be broken. If you want to make sure of keeping it intact, you must give your heart to no one, not even to an animal. Wrap it carefully round with hobbies and little luxuries; avoid all entanglements; lock it up safe in the casket or coffin of your selfishness. But in that casket—safe, dark, motionless, airless—it will change. It will not be broken; it will become unbreakable, impenetrable, irredeemable.

  C. S. Lewis, The Four Loves (1960).

- I think modern medicine has become like a prophet offering a life free of pain. It is nonsense. The only thing I know that truly heals people is unconditional love.

  Elisabeth Kübler-Ross, The Wheel of Life (1998).

- Love, from its awful throne of patient
    power
  In the wise heart, from the last giddy
    hour
  Of dread endurance, from the slippery,
    steep,
  And narrow verge of crag-like agony,
    springs
  And folds over the world its healing
    wings.

  Percy Bysshe Shelley, Prometheus Unbound (1820).

- Remember that children, marriages, and flower gardens reflect the kind of care they get.

  H. Jackson Brown, Jr. (ca. 2000; as cited by Hannah Doran, The Mum's Pocket Bible, 2010).

- It is the time you have wasted for your rose that makes your rose so important.

  Antoine de Saint-Exupéry, The Little Prince (1943, tr. Katherine Woods, 1943).

My love to you... sees your need to be loved when you have no time, and gives you time; hears your plea to be loved when you're out of breath, and lets you breathe; feels your beating heart when it's worked so hard, and brings you home.

We love because God first loved us.
— *John the Evangelist* [23]

---

[23] See page 96.

Facing page: J. Vold, Faith (2022).

9.

Faith

We love, as God loves us
    with Patience: God lives in us
    with Kindness: God shows
        through us
    with Generosity: God abides in us
    with Selflessness: God precedes us
    with Respect: God is here with us
    with Peace: God is perfected
        among us
    with Joy: God sings in us
    with Compassion: God is one of us
    with Faith: we are shown the way
    with Hope: we have no fear
    with Endurance: we are born of God
      for Eternity: we live by love.

- Beloved, let us love one another, because love is from God; everyone who loves is born of God and knows God. Whoever does not love does not know God, for God is love.

  ...So we have known and believe the love that God has for us. God is love, and those who abide in love abide in God, and God abides in them. Love has been perfected among us in this: that we may have boldness on the day of judgment, because as he is, so are we in this world.

  ...We love because he first loved us. Those who say, "I love God," and hate a brother or sister are liars; for those who do not love a brother or sister, whom they have seen, cannot love God whom they have not seen. The commandment we have from him is this: those who love God must love their brothers and sisters also.

  John the Evangelist, 1 John 4:7-8, 16-17, 19-21 (ca. 100, as cited by Anon., tr. NRSV, 2021).

- You shall love your neighbor as yourself.
  Moses, conveying God's commandments to the Israelites (ca. 1271 BC; as cited by Anon., Leviticus 19:18, ca. 332 BC, tr. NRSV, 2021).

- You shall not enter Paradise until you (truly) believe and you will not (truly) believe until you love each other.

  Muhammad (ca. 632; as cited by Abu Hurairah, ca., 680, in turn cited by Muslim ibn al-Hajjaj, Sahih Muslim, ca. 875, tr. Nasiruddin al-Khattab, 2007).

- When the Pharisees heard that [Jesus] had silenced the Sadducees, they gathered together, and one of them, an expert in the law, asked him a question to test him. "Teacher, which commandment in the law is the greatest?" He said to him, "'You shall love the Lord your God with all your heart and with all your soul and with all your mind.' This is the greatest and first commandment. And a second is like it: 'You shall love your neighbor as yourself.' On these two commandments hang all the Law and the Prophets."

  Jesus, with a lawyer (ca. 33, as cited by Anon., Matthew 22:34-40, ca. 95, tr. NRSV, 2021).

- Love is sustained by action, a pattern of devotion in the things we do for each other every day.

  Nicholas Sparks, The Wedding (2003).

- Love is an act of faith, and whoever is of little faith is also of little love.
  Erich Fromm, The Art of Loving (1956)

- Love is the active, working principle in all true faith. It is its very soul, without which it is dead. "Faith works by love."
  Jonathan Edwards (ca. 1758; as cited by Josiah Hotchkiss Gilbert, Dictionary of Burning Words of Brilliant Writers, 1895).

- There is always the danger that we may just do the work for the sake of the work. This is where the respect and the love and the devotion come in - that we do it to God, to Christ, and that's why we try to do it as beautifully as possible.
  Mother Teresa (ca. 1997; as cited by Christopher Locke, The Bombast Transcripts, 2002).

- It is love that asks, that seeks, that knocks, that finds, and that is faithful to what it finds.
  Augustine of Hippo (ca. 430; as cited by Josiah Hotchkiss Gilbert, Dictionary of Burning Words of Brilliant Writers , 1895).

- If you're lost, you can look and you will find me, time after time.
  Cyndi Lauper, Time After Time (1983).

• Love is no ingredient in a merely speculative faith, but it is the life and soul of a practical faith... A speculative faith consists only in the assent of the understanding, but in a saving faith there is also the consent of the heart.

> *Jonathan Edwards, Charity and Its Fruits (1738).*

• I cannot help thinking that the best way of knowing God is to love many things. Love this friend, this person, this thing, whatever you like, and you will be on the right road to understanding Him better, that is what I keep telling myself. But you must love with a sublime, genuine, profound sympathy, with devotion, with intelligence, and you must try all the time to understand Him more, better and yet more. That will lead to God, that will lead to an unshakeable faith.

> *Vincent van Gogh, Letter to Theo van Gogh (1880, tr. Johanna van Gogh-Bonger, ca.1925).*

• Love is seeing God in the person next to us, and meditation is seeing God within us.

> *Ravi Shankar, Wisdom for the New Millennium (2005).*

- You saw the best there was in me
Lifted me up when I couldn't reach
You gave me faith 'cause you believed
I'm everything I am
Because you loved me.
  Celine Dion, Because You Loved Me (1993).

- If it were so, ...that we should believe nothing that we cannot see with our physical eyes, then we first and foremost ought to give up believing in love.
  Søren Kierkegaard, Works of Love (1847, tr. Howard V. Hong and Edna H. Hong, 1995).

- I believe in the sun, though it be dark; I believe in God, though He be silent; I believe in neighborly love, though it be unable to reveal itself.
  Anon., inscribed in an underground room in Cologne; as reported by Neue Zürcher Nachrichten, 1945, tr. Nicholas Kontje, as cited by Everett Howe, ca. 2021.

- I believe it, nobody sold me
Always knew it, nobody told me
I believe in someone to hold me
I believe in love
  Kenny Loggins, Alan Bergman and Marilyn Bergman, I Believe in Love (1976, introduced by Barbra Streisand in A Star Is Born, then recorded by Kenny Loggins, 1977).

My love to you... believes in you, not just what I see in you but who I know you are to me: beautiful, made in the image of God and faithful to the original.

Love all men, even your enemies; love them, not because they are your brothers, but that they may become your brothers.

— *Augustine of Hippo* [24]

---

[24] See page 104.

Facing Page: J. Vold, Hope (2022).

10.

Hope

I hope to love you.
I love to hope
you will be my friend
when the fighting ends.

I hope to overcome
hate. I hope
that somehow enemies
can be friends.

I believe that love
may begin with hope
and that in that hope
love never ends.

I believe that we should
hold on to hope
for the end of hate
and the love of friends.

- Love all men, even your enemies; love them, not because they are your brothers, but that they may become your brothers.

  Augustine of Hippo, Sermon 10 on First John (407; as cited by Emile Mersch, The Whole Christ, tr. John R. Kelly, 1938).

- To love is to believe, to hope, to know; 'Tis an essay, a taste of Heaven below!

  Edmund Waller, Poems Upon Several Occasions (1693).

- Life and hope for the world are to be found only in the deeds of love.

  Bertrand Russell, Political Ideals (1917).

- I believe ... that dreams are more
      powerful than facts —
  That hope always triumphs over
      experience —
  That laughter is the only cure for grief.
  And I believe that love is stronger than
      death.

  Robert Fulghum, All I Really Need to Know I Learned in Kindergarten (1983).

- Behind the cloud the starlight lurks,
  Through showers the sunbeams fall;
  For God, who loveth all his works,
  Has left his Hope with all.

  John Greenleaf Whittier, A Dream of Summer (1847).

- There is a secret medicine given only to
  those who hurt so hard, they cannot
  hope.
  The hopers would feel slighted
  if they knew.
  Look as long as you can at the friend that
  you love, no matter whether that
  friend is moving away from you or
  coming back toward you.
  > Rumi (ca. 1273; tr. Coleman Barks, The
  > Essential Rumi, 1996).

- In strange and uncertain times, such as
  we're living through, sometimes a
  reasonable person might despair. But
  hope is unreasonable and love is greater
  even than this.
  > Robert Fripp, Interview with Mike Barnes,
  > Mojo Magazine (2013; restating a passage
  > from Robert Fripp's Diary, 2003).

- *PANDORA*
  What else remains for me?

  EPIMETHEUS
  Youth, hope, and love:
  To build a new life on a ruined life,
  To make the future fairer than the past,
  And make the past appear a troubled
  dream.
  > Henry Wadsworth Longfellow, The Masque of
  > Pandora (1875).

- Hope is a lover's staff; walk hence with
    that
  And manage it against despairing
    thoughts.
    *William Shakespeare, The Two Gentlemen of
    Verona (1590).*

- For every bird there is a stone thrown at
    a bird.
  For every loved child, a child broken,
    bagged,
  sunk in a lake. Life is short and the world
  is at least half terrible, and for every kind
  stranger, there is one who would
    break you,
  though I keep this from my children.
    I am trying
  to sell them the world. Any decent realtor,
  walking you through a real shithole,
    chirps on
  about good bones: This place could be
    beautiful,
  right? You could make this place
    beautiful.
    Maggie Smith, Good Bones (2016).

- If there is love, there is hope that one may
  have real families, real brotherhood, real
  equanimity, real peace.
    *Dalai Lama XIV, The Little Book of Buddhism
    (2000).*

- No one doubts that an ordinary man can get on with this world: but we demand not strength enough to get on with it, but strength enough to get it on. Can he hate it enough to change it, and yet love it enough to think it worth changing? Can he look up at its colossal good without once feeling acquiescence? Can he look up at its colossal evil without once feeling despair? Can he, in short, be at once not only a pessimist and an optimist, but a fanatical pessimist and a fanatical optimist? Is he enough of a pagan to die for the world, and enough of a Christian to die to it? In this combination, I maintain, it is the rational optimist who fails, the irrational optimist who succeeds. He is ready to smash the whole universe for the sake of itself.

  Gilbert K. Chesteron, Orthodoxy (1908).

- These dark days will be worth all they cost us if they teach us that our true destiny is not to be ministered unto but to minister to ourselves and to our fellow men.

  Franklin D. Roosevelt, Inaugural Address (1933).

- Love, hope, fear, faith — these make
  humanity;
  These are its sign and note and character.
  Robert Browning, Paracelsus (1835).

- You deserve a love that wants you disheveled, with everything and all the reasons that wake you up in haste, with everything and the demons that won't let you sleep.

  You deserve a love that makes you feel secure, able to take on the world when it walks with you, that feels your embraces are perfect for its skin.

  You deserve a love that wants to dance with you, that goes to paradise every time it looks into your eyes and never gets tired of studying your expressions.

  You deserve a love that listens when you sing, that supports you when you act like a fool, that respects your freedom; that accompanies you when you fly and isn't afraid to fall.

  You deserve a love that takes away the lies and brings you hope, coffee, and poetry.
  Estefanía Mitre, You Deserve a Love (2014, tr. Milton Fernandez, 2015).

My love to you... sees you before the sunrise and celebrates the new day even when it is still dark, knowing that the light will touch your face and reveal your beauty.

Lead a life worthy of the calling to which you have been called, with all humility and gentleness, with patience, bearing with one another in love, making every effort to maintain the unity of the Spirit in the bond of peace.

— *Paul the Apostle* [25]

---

[25] See page 112.

Facing Page: J. Vold, Endurance (2022).

11.

Endurance

Lead a life worthy of your calling:
Be patient, bearing one another in love;
Be kind, with all humility and gentleness;
Be giving, as each of us was given grace;
Be humble, by the measure of the gift;
Be respectful, to maintain the unity;
Be peaceful, and let peace be your bond;
Be joyful, of one body and one spirit;
Be caring, making every effort;
Believe in one God, one faith, one creed;
Be hopeful, just as you were called;
Be enduring, just as your call is to love;
And be always aware of the call.

- I therefore, the prisoner in the Lord, beg you to walk in a manner worthy of the calling to which you have been called, with all humility and gentleness, with patience, bearing with one another in love, making every effort to maintain the unity of the Spirit in the bond of peace.
  Paul the Apostle, Ephesians 4:1-3 (ca. 62, tr. NRSV, 2021).

- ...Lead a life worthy of the calling to which you have been called...
  Paul the Apostle, Ephesians 4:1 (ca. 62, tr. NRSV, 1989).

- "Love? What is love?" [Prince Andrey] thought.

  "...Love is life. All, everything that I understand, I understand only because I love. Everything is, everything exists, only because I love. Everything is united by it alone. Love is God, and to die means that I, a particle of love, shall return to the general and eternal source."
  Leo Tolstoy, War and Peace (1869, tr. Louise and Aylmer Maude, 1922).

- Love is the only thing that we can carry with us when we go, and it makes the end so easy.
  Louisa May Alcott, Little Women (1868).

- Love is not love
  Which alters when it alteration finds,
  Or bends with the remover to remove:
  O, no! it is an ever-fixed mark,
  That looks on tempests and is never
  shaken;
  William Shakespeare, Sonnet 66 (1609).

- We want with all our hearts to love, to be loved. And not just in the family but to look upon all as our mothers, sisters, brothers, children. It is when we love the most intensely and most humanly that we can recognize how tepid is our love for others. The keenness and intensity of love brings with it suffering, of course, but joy too, because it is a foretaste of heaven.
  Dorothy Day, On Pilgrimage (1997).

- Above all, maintain constant love for one another, for love covers a multitude of sins. Be hospitable to one another without complaining. Like good stewards of the manifold grace of God, serve one another with whatever gift each of you has received. Whoever speaks must do so as one speaking the very words of God; whoever serves must do so with the strength that God supplies...
  Peter the Apostle, 1 Peter 4: 8-11a (ca. 81, tr. NRSV, 2021).

- What is it that makes a person strong, stronger than the whole world; what is it that makes him weak, weaker than a child? What is it that makes a person unwavering, more unwavering than a rock; what is it that makes him soft, softer than wax? –It is love! What is it that is older than everything? It is love. What is it that outlives everything? It is love. What is it that cannot be taken but itself takes all? It is love. What is it that cannot be given but itself gives all? It is love. What is it that perseveres when everything falls away? It is love. What is it that comforts when all comfort fails? It is love. What is it that endures when everything is changed? It is love. What is it that remains when the imperfect is abolished? It is love. What is it that witnesses when prophecy is silent? It is love. What is it that does not cease when the vision ends? It is love. What is it that sheds light when the dark saying ends? It is love. What is it that gives blessing to the abundance of the gift? It is love. What is it that gives pith to the angel's words? It is love. What is it that makes the widow's gift an abundance? It is love.

    Søren Kierkegaard, Love Will Hide a Multitude of Sins (1843; tr. Howard V. Hong and Edna H. Hong, 1990).

- Endurance is patience concentrated.
  > *Thomas Carlyle (ca. 1881; as cited by Maturin M. Ballou, Edge-Tools of Speech, 1886).*

- Love knows no limit to its endurance, no end to its trust, no fading of its hope; it can outlast anything. It is, in fact, the one thing that still stands when all else has fallen.
  > *Paul the Apostle, 1 Corinthians 13:7-8a (ca. 56, tr. J. B. Phillips, 1958).*

- I *N.* take thee *N.* to my wedded wife, to have and to hold from this day forward, for better, for worse, for richer, for poorer, in sickness, and in health, to love and to cherish, til death us depart: according to God's holy ordinance: And thereto I plight thee my troth.
  > *Thomas Cranmer, Book of Common Prayer (1549).*

- Passion is momentary; love is enduring.
  > *John Wooden (ca. 2000, as cited by Cal Fussman, Coach!, UCLA Magazine, Summer 2000).*

- *FRANK CAPUA [as played by Paul Newman]* People stay married because they want to, not because the doors are locked.
  > *Howard Rodman, Winning (1969).*

- How do I love thee? Let me count the
   ways.
   I love thee to the depth and breadth and
   height
   My soul can reach, when feeling out of
   sight
   For the ends of Being and ideal Grace.
   I love thee to the level of everyday's
   Most quiet need, by sun and candlelight.
   I love thee freely, as men strive for Right;
   I love thee purely, as they turn from
   Praise.
   I love thee with the passion put to use
   In my old griefs, and with my childhood's
   faith.
   I love thee with a love I seemed to lose
   With my lost saints,—I love thee with the
   breath,
   Smiles, tears, of all my life! —and, if God
   choose,
   I shall but love thee better after death.
     Elizabeth Barrett Browning, Sonnets from the
     Portuguese, No. XLIII (1850).

- Juliet, when we made love you used to
   cry
   You said, "I love you like the stars above,
   I'll love you 'til I die."

   ...Juliet, I'd do the stars with you any time.
     Mark Knopfler, Romeo and Juliet (1980).

My love to you... vows forever and remembers its words, and when forever seems unrealistic and words are only words, my love, for however long it can, will live its promise.

My bounty is as boundless as the sea,
My love as deep; the more I give to thee,
The more I have, for both are infinite.
— *William Shakespeare* [26]

---

[26] See page 120.

Facing Page: J. Vold, Eternity (2022).

12.

Eternity

What's love? It's neither heart nor soul
Nor arm, nor face, nor any other part
belonging to the whole. O, be some other
    name!
What's in a name? That which we call love
By any other name would my heart beat;
So my love would, were it not love call'd,
Retain that dear perfection which it owes
Without that title. Call it so, or any name,
And of that name which is no part of thee
Take all myself.

     I take thee at thy word.
Call me but love, and I'll be new baptized.

- *JULIET*
What's Montague? It's neither heart nor
    soul
Nor arm, nor face, nor any other part
belonging to a man. O, be some other
    name!
What's in a name? That which we call a
    rose,
By any other word would smell as sweet.
So Romeo would — were he not Romeo
    call'd —
Retain that dear perfection which he owes
Without that title. Romeo, doff thy name,
And for that name, which is no part of
    thee,
Take all myself.

ROMEO
        [Aloud] I take thee at thy word.
Call me but love, and I'll be new
baptized...

...

JULIET
And yet I wish but for the thing I have;
My bounty is as boundless as the sea,
My love as deep; the more I give to thee,
The more I have, for both are infinite.
*William Shakespeare, Romeo and Juliet, Act.
2, Scene 2 (1600).*

- Till a' the seas gang dry, my dear,
And the rocks melt wi' the sun;
I will love thee still, my dear,
While the sands o' life shall run.

  And fare thee weel, my only luve!
And fare thee weel awhile!
And I will come again, my luve,
Though it were ten thousand mile.
  Robert Burns, A Red Red Rose

- Love rests on no foundation.
It is an endless ocean,
with no beginning or end.
  Rumi (ca. 1273, tr. Shahram Shiva, Hush Don't Say Anything to God, 1999).

- Love is the emblem of eternity; it confounds all notion of time; effaces all memory of a beginning, all fear of an end: we fancy that we have always possessed what we love, so difficult is it to imagine how we could have lived without it.
  Germaine de Staël, Corinne (1807, tr. Isabel Hill, 1833).

- The steadfast love of the Lord is from everlasting to everlasting.
  David, Psalm 103: 17 (ca. 1000 BC , as cited by Anon., Septuagint, ca. 247 BC, tr. NRSV, 2021).

- But love me for love's sake, that evermore
Thou may'st love on, through love's
  eternity.

> *Elizabeth Barrett Browning, Sonnets from the*
> *Portugese, No. XIV (1850).*

- If I could save time in a bottle
The first thing that I'd like to do
Is to save every day
'Til eternity passes away,
Just to spend them with you.

  If I could make days last forever;
  If words could make wishes come true;
  I'd save every day
  Like a treasure and then,
  Again, I would spend them with you.

  ...If I had a box just for wishes,
  And dreams that had never come true;
  the box would be empty,
  Except for the memory
  Of how they were answered by you.

  But there never seems to be enough time
  To do the things you want to do,
  Once you find them.
  I've looked around enough to know
  That you're the one I want to go
  Through time with.

> *Jim Croce, Time in a Bottle (1972).*

- Old sundial, you stand here for Time:
For Love, the vine that round your base
Its tendrils twines, and dares to climb
And lay one flower-capped spray in grace
Without the asking on your cold
Unsmiling and unfrowning face.
Yet, sundial, even Time may mould.
In years to come the foot shall stumble
Upon your shattered ruins where
This vine will flourish still, as rare,
As fresh, as fragrant as of old.
        Love will not crumble.

  Kisses have worn your stones away,
Lov'd lips you did not pulse beneath;
Dropt tears have hastened your decay
And brought you one step nigher death;
And you have heard, unthrilled,
    unmoved,
The music of Love's golden breath
And seen the light in eyes that loved.
You think you hold the core and kernel
Of all the world beneath your crust,
Old dial? But when you lie in dust,
This vine will bloom, strong, green, and
    proved.
Love is eternal.
Eleanor Farjeon, Time And Love (1908).

- If a thing loves, it is infinite.
William Blake, Annotations to Swedenborg (1788).

- Your God still walks in Eden, between the
    ancient trees,
  Where Youth and Love go wading
    through pools of primroses.
  And this is the sign we bring you, before
    the darkness fall,
  That Spring is risen, is risen again,
  That Life is risen, is risen again,
  That Love is risen, is risen again, and
    Love is Lord of all.
  > *Alfred Noyes, The Lord of Misrule (1915).*

- Ah, Christ, that it were possible,
  For one short hour to see
  The souls we loved, that they might tell
    us
  What and where they be.
  > *Alfred, Lord Tennyson, Maud (1855).*

- The truth is, indeed, that love is the
  threshold of another universe.
  > *Pierre Teilhard de Chardin, The Evolution of
  > Chastity (1936, tr. René Hague, 1975).*

- Love keeps us in Faith and Hope, and
  Hope leads us in Love. And in the end all
  shall be Love.
  > *Julian of Norwich, Revelations of Divine Love
  > (ca. 1393, tr. based on Grace Warrack, 1901).*

My love to you... will keep reminding you every day in as many ways as there are days, until every day becomes always and forever.

Love said to me,
there is nothing that is not me.
Be silent.

— *Rumi* [27]

---

[27] Rumi (ca. 1273, tr. Shahram Shiva, Hush Don't Say Anything to God, 1999).

Index

Love is patient;
Love is kind,
not envious but giving,
not boastful but selfless,
not arrogant but humble,
not rude but respectful
not insistent on its own way
but tolerant of others,
not irritable but peaceful,
not resentful but contented,
not taking pleasure in wrong-doing
but joyful about what is true.
Love carries the weight,
has faith in the future,
hopes for the best,
endures every day
and never goes away.
— Paul the Apostle [28]

---

[28] 1 Corinthians 13 (ca. 56, as paraphrased by J. Vold, 2022). See Chapters 1-12.

Love is
patient, kind, giving, humble, respectful,
peaceful, joyful, compassionate, faithful,
hopeful, enduring and always
from me
to you.